Amazing Medical People

Level 2
CEF A2–B1

D1585687

Text by
F.H. Cornish

Series edited by
Fiona MacKenzie

Collins

HarperCollins Publishers
77–85 Fulham Palace Road
Hammersmith London W6 8JB

10 9 8 7 6 5 4 3 2 1

Original text
© The Amazing People Club Ltd

Adapted text
© HarperCollins Publishers Ltd 2014

ISBN: 978-0-00-754509-4

Collins® is a registered trademark of
HarperCollins Publishers Limited

www.collinselt.com

A catalogue record for this book is available
from the British Library

Printed in the UK by Martins the Printers

These readers are based on original texts
(BioViews®) published by The Amazing
People Club group.® BioViews® and The
Amazing People Club® are registered
trademarks and represent the views of the
author.

BioViews® are scripted virtual interview
based on research about a person's life and
times. As in any story, the words are only
an interpretation of what the individuals
mentioned in the BioViews® could have
said. Although the interpretations are
based on available research, they do not
purport to represent the actual views of
the people mentioned. The interpretations
are made in good faith, recognizing that
other interpretations could also be made.
The author and publisher disclaim any
responsibility from any action that readers
take regarding the BioViews® for educational
or other purposes. Any use of the BioViews®
materials is the sole responsibility of the
reader and should be supported by their own
independent research.

Cover image © Studio 37/Shutterstock

✦ Contents ✦

Collins Amazing People Readers are collections of short stories. Each book presents the life story of five or six people whose lives and achievements have made a difference to our world today. The stories are carefully graded to ensure that you, the reader, will both enjoy and benefit from your reading experience.

You can choose to enjoy the book from start to finish or to dip into your favourite story straight away. Each story is entirely independent.

After every story a short timeline brings together the most important events in each person's life into one short report. The timeline is a useful tool for revision purposes.

Words which are above the required reading level are underlined the first time they appear in each story. All underlined words are defined in the glossary at the back of the book. Levels 1 and 2 take their definitions from the *Collins COBUILD Essential English Dictionary* and levels 3 and 4 from the *Collins COBUILD Advanced English Dictionary*.

To support both teachers and learners, additional materials are available online at www.collinselt.com/readers.

The Amazing People Club®

Collins Amazing People Readers are adaptations of original texts published by The Amazing People Club. The Amazing People Club is an educational publishing house. It was founded in 2006 by educational psychologist and management leader Dr Charles Margerison and publishes books, eBooks, audio books, iBooks and video content, which bring readers 'face to face' with many of the world's most inspiring and influential characters from the fields of art, science, music, politics, medicine and business.

◆ THE GRADING SCHEME ◆

The Collins COBUILD Grading Scheme has been created using the most up-to-date language usage information available today. Each level is guided by a brand new comprehensive grammar and vocabulary framework, ensuring that the series will perfectly match readers' abilities.

		CEF band	Pages	Word count	Headwords
Level 1	elementary	A2	64	5,000–8,000	approx. 700
Level 2	pre-intermediate	A2–B1	80	8,000–11,000	approx. 900
Level 3	intermediate	B1	96	11,000–15,000	approx. 1,100
Level 4	upper intermediate	B2	112	15,000–19,000	approx. 1,700

For more information on the Collins COBUILD Grading Scheme, including a full list of the grammar structures found at each level, go to www.collinselt.com/readers/gradingscheme.

Also available online: Make sure that you are reading at the right level by checking your level on our website (www.collinselt.com/readers/levelcheck).

Edward Jenner

◆◆◆

1749–1823

the man who fought the terrible disease, smallpox

When I was a child, I was 'variolated' at my school. This <u>treatment</u> protected me from a terrible disease called smallpox. But the treatment was very unpleasant. When I became a doctor, my <u>ambition</u> was to find a better way to protect people.

♦ ◆ ♦

I was born on 17th May 1749, at Berkeley, in the western part of England. My father was the priest at the church in Berkeley. When I was young, I went to schools which were near my home. Then, when I was 14 years old, I became an apprentice for seven years. I worked for a doctor in another town. I learnt from him the skills of a <u>surgeon</u> and the skills of a <u>family doctor</u>.

At that time, many people suffered from smallpox. Smallpox was a terrible disease. People who had it first had a <u>fever</u> and a <u>rash</u>, then pains in the head and back and stomach. After that, their bodies became covered with <u>blisters</u>. Many people who got smallpox died quickly.

When I was still at school, my friends and I were variolated. This treatment – variolation – protected people from smallpox. In fact, it gave people the disease, but the disease didn't kill them. I'll tell you how it was done. Some <u>pus</u> was taken from a blister on the body of someone who already had the disease. Then cuts were made in our arms and the pus was put under our skin. Then we were put in a building on our own and the door was locked. For several days we stayed there. We all became very ill. We had fevers and pains and we couldn't eat anything. It was terrible, but we didn't die.

When I became a doctor, I knew that <u>protection</u> against smallpox was important. I worked as a family doctor in Berkeley, and in this job I saw many people who had the disease. They hadn't been variolated, and the disease usually killed them. It often killed the people who looked after them too – their families and friends.

◆ ◆ ◆

One day, I met a woman called Catherine Kingscote. We fell in love and we were married in 1788. Catherine and I had three children. Now I had a problem – how could I protect *them* from smallpox? At that time in England, one child in every three children died of the disease. And we didn't have a useful treatment for it. I thought about variolation, but that treatment was horrible. I knew that from my own memories.

But was variolation the only answer to the problem? No, there was another answer. Some people who lived in villages in the countryside already knew about it. I'll tell you how *I* found out about it. In May 1796, a young woman called Sarah Nelmes came to see me. She worked on a farm, getting the milk from cows. She had a rash and I thought it might be a smallpox rash. I asked her, 'Have people in your village got the disease?' 'No,' she said. 'None of us has it, and none of us will get it, doctor. We've all had cowpox, and nobody who's had cowpox gets smallpox. I got cowpox from Blossom – she's one of the cows that I take milk from.'

'Is Sarah's story true?' I asked myself. Cowpox was a disease which cows often got, and people got it from them. It was a disease, but it wasn't as terrible as smallpox. People got a fever and some blisters, but they never died of cowpox. 'Can cowpox protect people against smallpox?' I asked myself.

I decided to test the idea and this is how I did it. A man who worked in my garden had a young son. The man was worried about his son. 'Will the boy get smallpox and die?' he asked me. I said that I had a new treatment and I wanted to test it. I could test it on his son. On 14th May 1796, I made cuts in the boy's arms and I put cowpox

pus under his skin. He had a fever for a short time, but it wasn't a bad one. Then on 1ˢᵗ July, I variolated him with smallpox pus. The treatment didn't make him ill.

I tried the test again with 23 other people. None of them became sick. Sarah Nelmes was right! People who'd had cowpox didn't get smallpox. And I quickly found out that I could take cowpox pus from people with the disease to <u>treat</u> other people. The pus didn't have to come from a cow each time.

I was pleased with my tests. When the news of them was printed in 1798, I was happy. Other British doctors could use my treatment, and we could stop the smallpox moving from one person to another – that's what I thought. But doctors who used variolation were unhappy. They wanted to use the treatment that they knew about. They didn't want to change. I hadn't got the <u>support</u> of my colleagues.

I soon found out that several other doctors, in different countries, had also tried the cowpox treatment. Like me, they hadn't got the support of their colleagues.

Some of our problems came from <u>religious</u> people. They thought that putting pus from animals into human bodies was wrong. 'God will be angry with you,' they said. But I thought that doctors could save millions of people's lives if they used my treatment. I called the treatment 'vaccination'. The name came from the Latin word *vacca*, which means 'cow'.

◆ ◆ ◆

Year after year, my work became more famous. The British government gave me money to help me with the work between 1802 and 1807. All my tests showed that Sarah Nelmes had been right.

Vaccination wasn't my only interest. I was very interested in the behaviour of birds and I spent a lot of time studying them. I wrote about that subject. But I'll always be remembered best for the work that I began after I talked to the farm girl, Sarah.

Vaccination with cowpox saved people's lives in Britain and in other parts of the world. People in France soon used my method of vaccination too, and later, doctors in other countries accepted it. In Britain, King George the Fourth gave me a job as Physician Extraordinary – a doctor for the royal family. I also became <u>Mayor</u> of Berkeley.

When I died on 26th January 1823, at the age of 73, there was still work to be done. But finally, during the 1840s, variolation was stopped in England, although vaccination was not made <u>compulsory</u> until 1853. I hoped that, one day, smallpox was going to disappear from the world.

The Life of Edward Jenner

1749   Edward Anthony Jenner was born in Berkeley, England, on 17th May.

1754   Both his parents died when Edward was 5 years old.

1757   Edward began his education. While he was at school, he was variolated – treated with smallpox to protect him from the disease.

1763   He started to work for a doctor called Daniel Ludlow.

1770   Edward went to London to study at Saint George's Hospital.

1773   Edward returned to Berkeley and became a family doctor.

1784   Edward became interested in birds and their behaviour. He studied the birds called cuckoos.

1788   His work was published in *Philosophical Transactions of the Royal Society*. He became a Fellow of the Royal Society. Edward married Catherine Kingscote. They later had three children.

1792   Edward studied medicine at the University of Saint Andrews, in Scotland.

1796   Edward discovered that he could protect a
       person from smallpox by using cowpox.

1798   Edward published his work on protection
       against smallpox.

1802   The British government gave Edward
       £10,000 to continue his work.

1805   He became a member of the Medical and
       Chirurgical Society. Later, the society's
       name changed to the Royal Society of
       Medicine.

1815   His wife, Catherine, died of the disease called
       tuberculosis.

1820   Edward had a serious illness of the brain, but
       he recovered.

1821   Edward became Physician Extraordinary to
       King George the Fourth. He also became
       the Mayor of Berkeley.

1823   He died on 26th January, in Gloucestershire,
       England.

Florence Nightingale

◆ ◆ ◆

1820–1910

the nurse known as 'the lady with the lamp'

My first name comes from a beautiful Italian city and my second name comes from a beautiful bird. But during my career, I saw many things that weren't beautiful. I saw soldiers with terrible <u>wounds</u>. I helped them, and other sick people, to <u>survive</u>.

◆ ◆ ◆

I was born on 12th May 1820, in Florence, Italy. My parents, who were English, lived in Italy at that time. I had a sister called Parthenope. Both of us were given the names of the places where we were born. My family moved back to England in the year after my birth. My father was a rich man and we had two large houses in the countryside. I grew up in these houses and I had my lessons at home. I enjoyed learning languages – I studied Latin, Greek, German, French and Italian.

When I was 17 years old, I decided that I wanted to work as a nurse. I didn't tell my parents at first. I knew that they didn't want girls from rich families like ours to work. But I looked at the poor people who lived near us. Their lives were very difficult and sad. The <u>Poor Laws</u> in England at that time were very cruel, and I wanted to improve them. And I cared about sick people and I wanted to help them. When I finally told my family this in 1844, my mother and sister were very unhappy. I knew what I wanted to do, but I hated upsetting my family.

I visited Kaiserswerth, in Germany, at about this time. There was a <u>training college</u> for nurses there. <u>Treatments</u> for sick people in England were bad, but in Kaiserswerth, I saw much better treatments.

When I returned to England, a man asked me to marry him. The man who wanted to marry me was a politician – a member of the British <u>parliament</u>. His name was Richard Monkton Milnes. Again, I upset my family when I refused to marry him. I didn't want to marry anyone.

♦ ◆ ♦

My health wasn't good, and my family were angry with me, so my health became worse. I wanted to leave England again. I spent some time in Rome, where I hoped to recover. During my stay there I met Sidney Herbert, another British politician. He became a close friend, and later he <u>supported</u> my <u>ambitions</u>.

In 1850, my family sent me to Egypt because my health was still not good. They hoped that warm, dry weather could help me. While I was there, I made some decisions about my future. I had no more doubts. I wanted to be a nurse. The next year I went back to Kaiserswerth. I began my <u>training</u> there.

When I returned to England in 1853, I started to <u>treat</u> sick women in London. My father didn't agree with my decision, but he supported me with money. Henry Manning, a famous priest, helped me too, and he became a good friend.

At this time, Britain was fighting Russia in the area called Crimea, on the north shore of the Black Sea. I heard sad news about the British soldiers who were fighting there. Many were <u>wounded</u> and many were sick. The treatment they received in the British military hospitals – the hospitals belonging to the army – wasn't good. I decided to help them. In October 1854, I took 38 other female nurses to Scutari, a town which is now part of Istanbul, in Turkey. Many wounded and sick British soldiers were in the British military hospital there. I saw the terrible <u>conditions</u> in the hospital and I quickly understood something. Many men were dying there, but their *wounds* weren't killing them. *Diseases* were killing them. Bad <u>hygiene</u> was the reason for this. The diseases called typhus, cholera and dysentery were killing the men because they had no fresh water to drink. And the disease called gangrene was killing them because their wounds weren't kept clean.

Most of the military doctors in the hospital didn't listen to our advice, because we were women. In fact, they made our work more difficult. But we began our nursing work and we washed the men's wounds and asked for better hygiene in the hospital. There were no antibiotics in those days, so we couldn't treat the men with <u>drugs</u>. But we changed their bandages regularly, and always kept new, clean ones for them. We were fighting a war within a war – a war against <u>infections</u>.

I often visited the men late at night. I carried a lamp and I looked carefully at each of my <u>patients</u>. People called me 'the lady with the lamp' – and they remembered that name for the rest of my life.

◆ ◆ ◆

We worked hard at Scutari, but 4,077 soldiers died during our first winter there. More of them died from infections *after* they were <u>wounded</u> than died because of their wounds. I collected <u>statistics</u> about this to show to the British government. The war had shown that the people in charge of the army had important medical problems to think about. I needed to support my ideas about hygiene, so I became a <u>statistician</u>.

When I returned to Britain, I was sick myself, and I had to stay in bed for a long time. But I didn't forget my work. My friend Sidney Herbert told me that Queen Victoria wanted my advice. I wrote a report – more than 1000 pages long – about my ideas. I sent the report to a <u>Royal Commission</u> which had been <u>established</u>. I thought that <u>preventing</u> infections was much better than treating them.

But how could we prevent infections? Diseases were a problem in Britain as well as in Crimea. Clean water for everyone and better <u>drains</u> were my two answers. Many people died from diseases after they drank water that wasn't clean. The <u>bacteria</u> that cause some diseases lived in the bad drains of our British towns and cities.

I continued to collect statistics about health. In 1858, I became the President of the Royal Statistical Society. The next year, I wrote two books – *Notes on Hospitals* and *Notes on Nursing*. Before I left Scutari, a Nightingale <u>Fund</u> had been established. A large amount of money – £45,000 – was given to this fund. I used the money to establish The Nightingale School of Nursing. This school opened in London in 1860. Nurses were <u>trained</u> in the school and they went to work in many parts of the country.

In my later years, I <u>campaigned</u> for better hygiene and for better training for nurses. But I also campaigned for women's <u>rights</u>. I wanted women to have good careers. Many people disagreed with me. They said, 'Women from rich families must stay at home.' But I continued with my work. And in 1869, my friend Elizabeth Blackwell and I established The Women's Medical College. I also wrote many more books, although most of them were not printed until after my death.

Slowly, people accepted my ideas about hygiene. Often the doctors in hospitals were the last people to accept them. But I worked to improve British nursing until 1895, when I became blind. And after I lost my sight, I was still interested in the improvements that were made by other people.

I died in London on 13th August 1910. I was 90 years old.

Two years after my death, a Florence Nightingale medal was created. It was given to nurses who did important work.

A Florence Nightingale medal

The Life of Florence Nightingale

1820   Florence was born at the Villa Colombaia, in Florence, Italy, on 12th May. Her parents were English.

1821   Her family returned to live in England.

1827   Florence's education began. She loved learning languages.

1837   She started to think about being a nurse.

1838   She began to tour Europe with her family.

1840   She returned to England with the family, and she attended Queen Victoria's birthday party.

1842   Florence met the politician Richard Monckton Milnes, who became her friend.

1844   She finally decided to become a nurse.

1847   Richard Monckton Milnes wanted to marry Florence. She refused, but they were still good friends. She met Sidney Herbert, another British politician, in Rome and he became her friend too.

1850   Florence continued her travels and visited Egypt and Greece. She also visited Kaiserswerth, in Germany, where her training as a nurse began the next year.

1853 She worked at the Institute for the Care of Sick Gentlewomen, in Upper Harley Street, London.

1854 Florence went to Scutari, in Turkey. Sidney Herbert asked her to nurse British soldiers who were wounded in the Crimean war. She was given the name, 'the lady with the lamp'.

1855 Florence established the Nightingale Fund, which raised money for the training of nurses. She became sick with an illness called 'Crimea Fever'.

1856 Florence wanted the government to study the health of the British Army. She was invited by Queen Victoria to give her views on the medical problems.

1857 A Royal Commission was established by the government to study nursing, but women were not allowed to be members of it. Florence sent her views to the commission.

1858 She was the first woman to become a member of the Royal Statistical Society.

1859 Florence published two books, *Notes on Nursing* and *Notes on Hospitals*.

1860   Florence established the Nightingale
       Training School for nurses at Saint Thomas's
       Hospital, London.

1869   She established the Women's Medical
       College in London with the doctor
       Elizabeth Blackwell. Elizabeth believed in
       the rights of women.

1883   Florence was given a medal — the Royal
       Red Cross — by Queen Victoria.

1895   Florence's health became worse and she lost
       her sight.

1907   Florence became the first woman to receive
       the Order of Merit from the British king,
       Edward the Seventh.

1910   Florence died in London, aged 90, on
       13th August.

Elizabeth Garrett Anderson

◆ ◆ ◆

1836–1917

England's first female doctor

I was the first English woman to work as a doctor in my own country. During my long life, I tried to improve the lives of women. And I helped to create Britain's first medical school for women.

◆ ◆ ◆

I was born in Whitechapel, East London, on 9th June 1836. I was the second of my parents' 11 children. My father, Newson Garrett, worked for a company that bought and sold jewellery. He also made silver jewellery himself. But he wasn't a Londoner. His family lived in Suffolk, in the eastern part of England. They lived in a small town called Leiston, and my father was born there. His family owned a factory in Leiston that made things from iron. My father had two brothers who worked for the company, so he decided to have a different career.

My father was successful and he earned a lot of money in London. But when I was about 5 years old, he decided to move back to Suffolk. He bought a company that sold coal and also <u>barley</u>. My father built a large factory in Snape, which was a few miles from Leiston. The workers in the factory <u>malted</u> the barley.

My father paid for a good education for all his sons and daughters. But when I left school, I became interested in feminism – the <u>rights</u> of women. I met a young woman called Emily Davies who was also a feminist. We wanted men and women to have equal rights. We talked about that a lot. My <u>ambition</u> was to become a doctor. But at that time, there were no women doctors in England. I wanted to be a student at a medical school, but none of the medical schools accepted me. They told me that women could never be doctors.

I couldn't study to be a doctor in England, so I decided to become a student *nurse* in London. I began to learn about medicine in the hospital where I <u>trained</u>. I was sometimes allowed to watch the doctors while they worked. But I wanted to be a doctor myself, not a nurse. I couldn't take examinations to <u>qualify</u> as a doctor at an English medical school. I decided to try something different.

There was a Society of Apothecaries in London. Apothecaries prepared <u>drugs</u> and gave them to sick people. They often worked as <u>family doctors</u>. But they weren't <u>surgeons</u> – they didn't <u>operate</u> on people. The society held examinations for people who wanted to become apothecaries. And the rules of their society didn't stop women taking their examinations. So I joined the society and worked as an *apprentice* apothecary for five years – now I was training to be an apothecary.

During that time, I visited Scotland. English medical schools weren't helpful to me. But the medical schools in the Scottish universities were more helpful to women. Doctor Day, the Professor of Medicine at Saint Andrew's University, allowed me to listen to lectures with the male students. Doctor Simpson, in Edinburgh, also helped me. I learned things in Scotland that I couldn't learn in England. But some of the teachers there refused to teach me too. One of them wrote that ladies could only be bad doctors, so there was no need for them.

I returned to London, and I continued to work as a nurse in hospitals there. The <u>conditions</u> were terrible. Surgeons operated on people without any <u>hygiene</u>. Many of the <u>patients</u> got <u>infections</u> and died. I wanted to make <u>operations</u> safer for them.

◆ ◆ ◆

In 1865, after my time as an apprentice finished, I was ready to qualify as an apothecary. But suddenly, there was a problem. The Society of Apothecaries tried to stop me taking their examinations. My father said that he was going to <u>sue</u> the society, and it knew that he had a strong argument. So I was allowed to answer the examination questions. I passed the examinations and I qualified as an apothecary. The society changed its rules after that, so that women *couldn't* take their examinations. But the society couldn't take away my qualification. So, at last, I was a sort of doctor.

I was still not able to work as a doctor in any British hospital. But my father helped me to establish a dispensary for women in London. I was able to treat women's illnesses there. And fortunately, I met some people who had the same ideas about women's problems. One of them, Elizabeth Blackwell, had qualified as a doctor in America. The two of us established several medical centres for women. And also in 1865, my friend Emily Davies and I established the Kensington Society with some other women. This was a society of feminists.

At that time, women couldn't vote in elections in Britain. We wanted women to be able to vote so we sent a petition – a document signed by a lot of people – to the British government. But the government didn't listen to us. As a result, a new society – the National Union of Women's Suffrage Societies – was created. 'Suffrage' was the right to vote. Women who wanted this right were called 'suffragettes'.

One person who listened to our ideas was a man called Henry Fawcett. He was a member of the British parliament, and he was blind. He invited me to have dinner with him one day, and after that we often met. I liked him a lot, and soon he asked me to marry him. I didn't want to do that, but we stayed friends. Later,

Henry married Millicent, one of my sisters. Millicent later became a very famous suffragette.

My main ambition was still to help women and children who were ill. Many poor people came to my dispensary for help and advice. But I needed to qualify as a hospital doctor to do the work that I wanted to do in England.

The English medical schools still refused to teach women. But in France, it *was* possible for women to study in medical schools. So I learned some French and I travelled to France. And at the University of Paris, I earned a medical degree at last.

After that, I thought that I could start my medical career in England. But I was wrong. All doctors had to be members of the British Medical Register if they worked in British hospitals. This was a list of people who were qualified as hospital doctors. The men who controlled the Register refused to accept my French qualification.

Now I knew that qualifications weren't enough. Political changes were needed too. So I had to become a well-known person and then to fight for my ideas. First, I became <u>involved</u> in education. In 1870, I was <u>elected</u> to the East London School Board. This was a group of people who controlled education in the East London area. I was the first woman who was ever elected to a school board in England.

A man called James Anderson was involved in my election <u>campaign</u>. He worked for the Orient Steamship Company, and he was very successful businessman. We became very close and in 1871, we were married. After that, I was called Elizabeth Garrett Anderson – that is the name most people now remember.

James and I had three children together – two girls and a boy. Unfortunately, one of our daughters died when she was very young.

◆ ◆ ◆

I already had my dispensary. Then in 1872, I decided to change it into a hospital – the New Hospital for Women. I had to collect money and find a new building. And I had to find staff – people to work there. But it was my own hospital, so all the staff were women when the hospital opened in 1874. Before that happened, in 1873, I became the first woman member of the British Medical Association. It was 19 years before there was another female member of that society, because the Association changed its rules after I joined. Most British doctors didn't want women to join them.

While I worked at the hospital, I continued with my political work. I wanted politicians to give women more opportunities. Talking to politicians was hard work, but in 1876 my feminist friends and I had a great success. In that year, the British parliament passed a new law. It allowed women in Britain to qualify as doctors and to be listed on the Medical Register. This new law encouraged girls to study medical subjects. Universities began to establish more medical courses as a result. Change was slow, but it happened.

◆ ◆ ◆

In 1883, I became the head of the London School of Medicine. By now I knew that people needed more than medicine and doctors to improve their lives. People's living conditions had to change. Poor people lived in awful houses. Often, many people lived in one room. The <u>drains</u> in the large cities were very bad. Diseases were common in conditions like these. I tried to improve conditions for the people who came to me for advice.

I continued my fight until I stopped working as a doctor. Then in 1902, when I was 66, we moved back to Suffolk. We lived in Aldeburgh, a small town on the coast. It was only a few miles from Leiston and Snape and it was a place which I knew well from my childhood. We became involved in Suffolk politics. My husband became the <u>Mayor</u> of Aldeburgh. We tried to improve conditions for the poor people of the town. James died in 1907, but the people of the town elected me as their next mayor. I became the first female mayor in England. But I was still interested in national politics, and in feminism.

I became a member of the Women's Social and Political Union and I often joined the suffragettes in London. We wanted votes for women and we complained about the government. We stood and shouted outside government buildings and we didn't let the politicians forget about us.

Because of my age, the police didn't arrest me. But many suffragettes *were* arrested and sent to prison. My daughter Louisa, like me, was a doctor and a suffragette. I was proud of her. We fought together for women's rights and for children's rights. Although some suffragettes believed that only violence could change the government's ideas, I didn't agree. Those women broke windows and damaged buildings, but I tried always to use peaceful arguments.

When I died, on 17th December 1917, I'd lived a long and useful life. By then, there were many woman doctors in Britain. And 11 years after my death, all British women over the age of 21 finally got the vote.

The Life of Elizabeth Garrett Anderson

1836   Elizabeth Garrett was born on 9th June, in Whitechapel, London. She was one of 11 children born to Newson Garrett and his wife, Louisa.

1841   The family moved to Suffolk. Her father became a successful businessman in Snape.

1849   At the age of 13, Elizabeth went away to school.

1854   Elizabeth met Emily Davies, a young feminist, while visiting a friend in London.

1859   Elizabeth met Elizabeth Blackwell, the first woman in the United States to qualify as a doctor. Elizabeth decided that she also wanted a career in medicine.

1860   Elizabeth became a student nurse at the Middlesex Hospital in London. She also became an apprentice apothecary.

1865   She qualified as the first British woman apothecary. Elizabeth helped to form a feminist group called the Kensington Society.

1866   Elizabeth established the Saint Mary's
       Dispensary for Women and Children. She
       went to study at the University of Paris.

1870   Elizabeth passed the examinations and
       qualified as a doctor in Paris. She wasn't
       allowed to join the British Medical Register,
       but she became a visiting doctor at the East
       London Hospital.

1871   Elizabeth married James Skelton Anderson, a
       successful businessman. She became Elizabeth
       Garrett Anderson. Elizabeth and James had
       three children, Louisa, Margaret and Alan.
       Margaret died when she was very young.

1872   Elizabeth opened the New Hospital for
       Women in London. The doctors and nurses
       were women and so were the patients.
       Elizabeth Blackwell was one of the doctors
       who worked there.

1873   Elizabeth became a member of the British
       Medical Association.

1874   Elizabeth and her friends established the
       London School of Medicine for Women.

1876   The British parliament finally made a law
       that allowed women to qualify as doctors in
       British medical schools.

1883   Elizabeth became head of the London
       School of Medicine.

1889   She became a member of the Central Committee of the National Society for Women's Suffrage.

1897   Elizabeth was elected President of the British Medical Association in the East of England.

1902   She retired from medicine and she returned to Suffolk. She lived in Aldeburgh. Elizabeth continued her interest in politics there.

1907   Elizabeth's husband died.

1908   Elizabeth was elected Mayor of Aldeburgh. She was Britain's first woman mayor. She also became a member of the Women's Social and Political Union.

1917   Elizabeth died in Suffolk on 17th December, aged 81. The London School of Medicine for Women became the Elizabeth Garrett Anderson Hospital. It is now part of the University of London.

Carl Jung

◆ ◆ ◆

1875–1961

the doctor who wanted to understand the
human mind

I was a doctor, but my main interest was in people's minds, not their bodies. My <u>ambition</u> was to help people who had <u>personality</u> problems. I tried to understand their minds. I became a kind of <u>philosopher</u> as well as a doctor.

◆ ◆ ◆

I was born in Kesswil, in Switzerland, on 26ᵗʰ July 1875. My father was a priest who worked in the countryside and in small villages. I was the fourth child of my parents, but I was the only one who lived to be an adult.

When I was young, my parents taught me about their <u>religious</u> <u>beliefs</u>. My mother believed in God, but she was very unhappy. She suffered from <u>depression</u>. She often stayed in her bedroom all day. She said that spirits – ghosts – visited her in the night and talked to her. I became very interested in these strange events when I was a child. They were called 'occult phenomena'.

I was always a thoughtful child and I spent a lot of time alone, thinking about myself. I decided that I had two <u>identities</u>. One was the identity of a shy schoolboy who lived in the nineteenth century – the person who my friends and family knew. But I also had the identity of a much older person from the eighteenth century. This other identity was someone who was powerful and clever. He was someone whose words people believed. I thought that I could help other people in their lives because of this powerful second identity.

One day at school, another boy knocked me over and I was <u>unconscious</u> for a short time. For the next six months I didn't attend school. Every time I thought about school, or tried to do some schoolwork, I became unconscious again. I stopped thinking about my future and I let my fears control my life. Later in my life, this event helped me to understand neurosis, a <u>mental condition</u> that makes people worried and afraid for a long period of time. But when I was young, it was my father who helped me to deal with my problem.

One day, I heard my father talking to someone else about me. He said that he was worried about me. He thought that I would never be able to get a job and earn money for myself. And he was worried because he didn't earn enough money to help me. At that moment I understood that my father was a poor man. He never talked to me about that. And I understood that I had to continue with my education and find a career for myself.

My main ambition at that time was to become an architect, but the University of Basel, near our home, didn't teach that subject. Instead, I studied to become a doctor.

I studied medicine at Basel from 1895 to 1900. During this time, I became very interested in psychiatric medicine – treatments for people with mental illnesses. Unfortunately, my father died the year after I began my medical studies.

After I qualified as a family doctor, I studied for another degree at the University of Zurich. My teacher there was a famous psychiatrist called Eugen Bleuler. The thesis that I completed after my three years, study with him was about occult phenomena. The thesis was published – it was my first book. And after that, I published many books and articles during my long life.

◆ ◆ ◆

During the next few years, I met two people who became very important in my life. As a result of the first meeting, in 1903 I married a woman called Emma Rauschenbach. She was a member of one of the richest families in Switzerland. Emma and I had five children, and we were married for more than 50 years. And in 1906, I sent a copy of my new book, *Studies in Word Association* to Sigmund Freud. Freud, the famous Viennese doctor who developed psychoanalysis, was twenty years older than me. Psychoanalysis is the treatment of someone who has mental problems by talking about their past life and their feelings. Freud was very interested in my book. When we met, the next year, we talked for many hours. Between that year and 1913, we wrote to each other frequently and worked on various problems of psychology together.

Together, Freud and I developed many ideas about human behaviour. But by 1913, there were differences between us. Freud was convinced that libido – sexual energy – was the most important factor in human development. I thought that it was one important factor, but certainly not the *only* important factor. Also our ideas about the psychology of religion were very different. I thought that humans had a need to believe in something – that they were born with this need. Freud wasn't interested in religion at all and he disagreed with me. I explained what I thought in my book, *Psychology of the Unconscious*, and when it was published in 1912, Freud and I argued about it. The next year, we stopped working together.

◆ ◆ ◆

In 1914, the First World War began and during the next four years millions of people died. Switzerland was a neutral country – it didn't fight on either side. But it was a time of stress for everyone. I started to work as an analyst – a doctor who treats people with mental problems. I had many <u>patients</u> who'd lost their interest in life. I treated them by talking to them. They told me about their fears and they told me about their dreams.

I learned a lot from my patients. Then, in the years after the war, I studied people's cultures and their languages. My wife was rich, so we were able to travel. We travelled in many European countries. We also went to North Africa, Kenya, the USA and India. During those travels I found many links between different peoples and different cultures.

I became very interested in Eastern <u>philosophies</u>. They increased my feeling that people's beliefs were important. I was already <u>involved</u> in medicine, psychology and psychiatry but now I became interested in <u>archaeology</u> too. But treating patients with mental problems was always my main ambition.

When I returned to Switzerland, I had more and more patients. They were all trying to understand their lives. No technologies, no <u>drugs</u>, and no prayers could solve their problems. But I helped them to understand their thoughts and their behaviour.

I asked my patients about their present lives and their future wishes, instead of talking always about the past with them, like Freud did. I wanted them to ask themselves, 'Who *am* I?' And I wanted them to ask, 'Where am I going?'

Freud had written a lot about the <u>unconscious mind</u>, but I thought that his understanding of it was too simple.

I thought that people had a 'personal unconscious', which was only theirs. But I thought that there was also a 'collective unconscious' which was shared by all people. I thought that an analyst needed to work with both of these types of unconscious mind. And I also thought about the groups of people that <u>psychologists</u> called <u>introverts</u> or <u>extroverts</u>. This also was too simple. There were different types of personality within these groups. Examples of these are 'thinking types' and 'feeling types'.

So, over the years, I helped people to find personal answers to their problems. I helped them to understand their lives, sometimes by thinking about different philosophies and religions. I helped them to accept the

The C.G. Jung Institute in Zurich

negative parts of their own personalities. By doing all this, I developed my personal method of treatment – analytical psychology. This was very different from Freud's psychoanalysis. In 1948, I established the C.G. Jung Institute in Zurich. This college trained many analysts to use my methods.

My work took me into many mental worlds – the worlds of dreams and mythology, the worlds of religion and philosophy, the worlds of art and alchemy. I wasn't the type of doctor who used medical drugs – I tried to give equal importance to science and belief for each patient.

I never retired. My analytic work, and the many books that I wrote, kept me busy until my death on 6th June 1961. One of my last books was an autobiography – the story of my life.

The Life of Carl Jung

1875   Carl Gustav Jung was born in Kesswil, Switzerland, on 26th July.

1879   His mother, Emilie, suffered from depression and the Jung family moved closer to her family in Kleinhuningen, Basel.

1887   During his teenage years, Carl was often unwell. He became unconscious many times when he thought about his school.

1895   He attended the University of Basel and studied medicine there.

1896   His father, Paul, died.

1900   Carl became an assistant doctor at a psychiatric hospital, the Burgholzli Hospital, Zurich.

1902   He completed his Master's degree at the University of Zurich and published his thesis, *On the Psychology and Pathology of So-Called Occult Phenomena.*

1903   He married Emma Rauschenbach and they later had five children.

1905   Carl lectured in psychiatry at the University of Zurich.

1906   Carl's *Studies in Word Association* was
        published. He sent this to Sigmund Freud
        in Vienna.

1907   Carl met Sigmund Freud and they had many
        conversations.

1909   Carl travelled to America with Sigmund
        Freud and the Hungarian psychoanalyst,
        Sándor Ferenczi.

1910   Carl became a leader of the International
        Psychoanalytical Association.

1912   Carl published *Psychology of the Unconscious*.
        He had arguments with Freud because of
        this book. After this, they were not close
        friends.

1914   During the First World War, Carl worked
        as an army doctor. He left the International
        Psychoanalytic Association.

1923   Carl's mother, Emilie, died.

1924   Carl travelled to Taos in New Mexico,
        where he studied the Pueblo Indians.

1925   Carl travelled to East Africa and studied the
        people of Mount Elgon in Kenya.

1933   He was leader of the International part of the
        General Medical Society for Psychotherapy.
        He also became Professor of Psychology at
        the Federal Polytechnic University of Zurich.

1937   During a tour of India, Carl became seriously ill. He spent two weeks in a hospital.

1942   He retired from The Federal Polytechnic University of Zurich.

1944   Carl was Professor of Medical Psychology at the University of Basel. His book *Psychology and Alchemy* was published.

1948   The C.G. Jung Institute in Zurich was established.

1955   Carl's wife, Emma, died in Zurich.

1957   He began writing his autobiography *Memories, Dreams, Reflections*, which was published two years after his death.

1959   *Flying Saucers: A Modern Myth of Things Seen in the Skies* was published.

1961   Carl died on 6th June in Kusnacht, Zurich, after a short illness. He was 85 years old.

Jonas Salk

◆ ◆ ◆

1914–1995

the man who defeated the dangerous illness, polio

Find out where the enemy lives. Study how the enemy behaves. Find out how the enemy's numbers increase. Then attack the enemy! That was what I told myself, and that was my method during my life as a scientist. For me, the enemy was a disease.

◆ ◆ ◆

I was born on 28th October 1914, in New York City, USA. My parents were Jewish Russians, but they moved to America to find a better life. They learned a new language and a new kind of life. I had two brothers and a sister, and my parents worked hard to give us all a good home.

When I <u>graduated</u> from high school, my parents wanted me to attend college. At first, I planned to study law at City College in New York. But I was more interested in science than in law, so I decided to study medicine. I attended the New York Medical School and <u>qualified</u> as a doctor there. And in 1939, I married a girl called Donna Lindsay.

At that time, in the later 1930s, there was a terrible <u>depression</u> in America. Many people were very poor. Many people didn't have jobs. Many people were ill. I wanted to help people. But I decided not to become a <u>family doctor</u>. I decided to work in medical research. I wanted to study <u>viruses</u>.

After I qualified, I worked for a short time with Doctor Thomas Francis in Michigan. We wanted to find a <u>vaccine</u> to protect people against flu. Good progress was made on that project, but the work stopped for a while because of the Second World War. In those years, it was more important to do other projects. But later, we worked on flu again for the US Army.

◆ ◆ ◆

After the war, I moved to Pittsburgh and worked at the university there. At this time, my interest was in a vaccine against poliomyelitis. Polio, as it was usually called, was a terrible disease. It could <u>cripple</u> people and it could kill people. It could attack young people and old people. The disease had been <u>identified</u> in 1789. But 150 years later, it still crippled and killed millions of people. In 1952, in the USA, more than 21,000 people died as a result of polio. Some people who had the disease <u>survived</u>, but had to live in a machine that helped them to breathe. Others were able to live better lives, but with weak limbs. These people were often unable to move their legs properly so they couldn't live normal lives.

Polio was my enemy. Day after day, and night after night, I saw the enemy at work. The disease was caused by a virus – I knew that. A man called Landsteiner had identified the virus in 1908. But I needed to know how the virus worked. I also needed to know how it moved from one person to another. Then perhaps I could find a vaccine that could stop the disease from doing this.

Perhaps an answer to my problem was immunization – protecting people by giving them <u>injections</u>. This had been successful with other diseases. Was it possible to protect people from a serious attack of polio by giving them a form of the disease which wasn't serious? I thought that this might be the correct answer to my problem, but lots of work was needed on the virus.

From 1950, it was possible to grow the virus in a laboratory because of the work of two other doctors. It was now possible to have large amounts of the virus to work on. I worked on this 'laboratory virus' and I found something useful. I found that the <u>chemical</u> called formaldehyde made the virus much weaker. 'If I <u>inject</u> this very weak virus into healthy people, will it protect them from getting polio?' I asked myself. I tested the idea by injecting animals. It worked – the animals didn't become sick and they didn't get polio. Next I needed to test the injection on people.

I knew that the danger from a serious polio attack was much worse than the danger from my very weak laboratory virus. So I asked my wife Donna, 'Can I inject you and our three sons?' She agreed and I injected them, and also myself. None of us became ill.

I wanted to protect healthy people from polio. But I also wanted to improve the lives of people who already had the disease. I was able to inject some children who already had polio. The injections were successful. They made the lives of the children better. It was time to offer the <u>treatment</u> to many more people.

◆ ◆ ◆

By 1954, <u>vaccinations</u> had begun in the USA. Doctor Thomas Francis from Michigan was very helpful to me again. As a result, two million children, aged 6–9, were <u>involved</u>. And this was only the start.

Two years later, the number of people who got polio in the USA had fallen by 85 percent. The number of deaths from the disease fell, too. And by 1959, the vaccination was used in more than 90 countries.

In 1961, a man called Doctor Albert Sabin made a new kind of vaccine. It was an oral vaccine – it was put in <u>patients</u>' mouths and they swallowed it, so there wasn't an injection. This made it much easier to give the vaccine to children. Together, we were beating the enemy.

◆ ◆ ◆

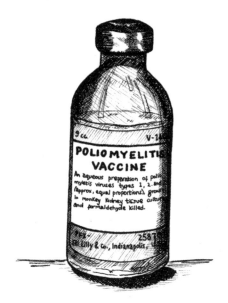

There was still a lot of work to do. That's why, in the 1960s, I <u>established</u> a new laboratory – The Salk Institute for Biological Studies in La Jolla, California. We worked on treatments for many diseases there. By 1994, there was no poliomyelitis in the USA. But there was still a lot of polio in four countries – Nigeria, India, Pakistan, and Afghanistan. So the fight continued. My own research in my later years was on treatments for the HIV virus, which causes the disease called AIDS. That virus became a big problem around the world.

Disease will always be the enemy. Medical people will always have to fight against new diseases. But when I died, on 23ʳᵈ June 1995, I knew that I'd made the world a better place.

The Life of Jonas Salk

1914   Jonas Edward Salk was born on 28th October in New York City, USA. His parents, Daniel and Dora, were from Russia.

1921   Franklin D. Roosevelt, who later became the American president, became ill with poliomyelitis. Many people in the world had this disease in the early twentieth century.

1930   Jonas started to study law at the City College of New York. Then he decided to study medicine instead.

1934   Jonas graduated with a Bachelor of Science degree and started to study at The New York University School of Medicine.

1939   Jonas graduated from the New York University School of Medicine. He worked with Doctor Thomas Francis in Michigan, on research into flu. Jonas married Donna Lindsay and they later had three children.

1940   Jonas worked as a doctor at Mount Sinai Hospital in New York.

1941   He went to the University of Michigan
       to continue his work in virology. He was
       taught by Doctor Thomas Francis, and
       worked in his laboratory. Jonas and Doctor
       Francis developed a flu vaccine which was
       used by the US Army.

1944   Jonas became Research Associate in
       Epidemiology.

1947   He became the Director of the Virus
       Research Laboratory at the University of
       Pittsburgh.

1950   Two scientists, Doctor William Hammon
       and Doctor Enders, found important new
       information in work on the polio virus. As a
       result, Jonas developed a vaccine.

1954   National testing of the vaccine began.

1955   Doctor Francis studied the vaccine and
       found that it was safe and that it worked.
       After that, the Salk Vaccine was used in
       every part of the USA.

1956   President Eisenhower gave Jonas a
       Congressional Medal for Distinguished
       Civilian Service. By the following year, over
       100 million people were injected with the
       vaccine.

1962–1963 Polio was not a big problem any longer. Building began at The Salk Institute for Biological Studies in La Jolla, California. The first laboratory opened in 1963.

1968 Jonas and Donna's marriage ended.

1970 Jonas married Françoise Gilot. She had been a friend and model for the artist, Pablo Picasso.

1972 *Man Unfolding* was published, followed by *The Survival of the Wisest*, one year later.

1976 Jonas was named American Humanist of the Year.

1977 President Jimmy Carter gave Jonas the Presidential Medal of Freedom.

1985 President Ronald Reagan named 6th May as Jonas Salk Day in the USA.

1993 China started a national project to vaccinate people against polio and over the next few years, other countries did the same.

1994 By now, there was no more polio in America.

1995 Jonas died on 23rd June in La Jolla, California, USA. He was 80 years old.

Christiaan
Barnard

* ◆ *

1922–2001

the first man to replace a human heart

I became a doctor because I had a special <u>ambition</u>. My ambition was to give seriously ill people some extra years of life. For this reason, I became a heart <u>surgeon</u>. I became the first surgeon to <u>transplant</u> a human heart.

◆ ◆ ◆

I was born on 8th November 1922, in Beaufort West. Beaufort West is a town in the Karoo region of South Africa. My father was a missionary in the Dutch Reformed Church there – he taught people about religion. I had four brothers, but one of them died when he was very young. His name was Abraham and he died of <u>heart failure</u>. That was when I realized that human life is special, and our time on Earth is special.

I had lots of time to think about this because each day, I had to walk to school. Our home was more than two miles from the school. My father was a kind man, and he taught me about kindness. But my mother taught me about ambition. I worked very hard at school, because I wanted to become a doctor – my ambition was to be a surgeon.

I graduated from Beaufort West High School in 1940, and I went to study medicine at the University of Cape Town. By 1946, I had qualified as a doctor. First I worked at the Groote Schuur Hospital in Cape Town, then I worked as a family doctor in a small town in the province. During this time I met Aletta Louw. Aletta was a nurse, and we liked each other immediately. By 1948, we were married and we started our family. We had two children, Andre and Deirdre.

In 1951, we moved back to Cape Town, where I gained a Master of Medicine degree in 1953. The same year, I completed a thesis about the disease called tuberculous meningitis. I earned another degree because I had written that thesis.

◆ ◆ ◆

I started to work long hours at the Groote Schuur Hospital. This was when I became interested in the pump that we call the human heart. Memories of my brother's death from a heart problem had never left me. 'How can I help other people with heart problems?' I asked myself. I wanted to learn more, so in 1956 I went to the USA to study heart surgery.

It was an exciting time, because new ideas about heart surgery were talked about in America. Doctor Norman Shumway and his colleagues were helpful to me. I wrote another thesis about a part of the heart called the aortic valve.

We discovered that we could probably replace diseased hearts, because of research with animals. But, many people didn't want doctors to replace human hearts. This was strange. For a number of years doctors had replaced other organs in the human body. Perhaps people could change their minds about hearts.

◆ ◆ ◆

When I returned to South Africa, I began to work on kidney transplants. In 1959, I did the first kidney transplants in South Africa. I was taking organs from dead people to give to living people. By doing this, I was keeping people alive. 'If it isn't wrong to transplant other organs, why is it wrong to transplant hearts?' I asked myself. Some people who didn't like the idea of heart transplants were religious people. And some of them were politicians. These people's reasons weren't medical ones. But some of my medical friends were unhappy about heart transplants too.

I did more tests with animals. The transplant operations were successful for a time, although the animals died later. The main problem was rejection – the animal's body could not accept the new heart.

I needed to test my ideas on a human. Louis Washkansky, a man aged 53, was dying from heart failure in my hospital. He couldn't live much longer. He agreed to have a heart transplant. Now we waited for a <u>patient</u> with a good heart to die from some other problem.

On 3rd December 1967, Denise Darvall died at the hospital. She was very badly hurt in a car crash, and she died soon after the accident. The transplant operation took five hours, with a team of 30 people – doctors and nurses. We took Denise's heart and transplanted it into Louis's body. The operation was a success, but only for a short time. Louis lived for 18 days, then his body rejected the new heart and he died.

The world's newspapers, radio and TV stations heard about the transplant. Suddenly, I was famous. The operation gave hope to many people, but we had to solve the problem of rejection. Then we could save the lives of many dying people.

On 2nd January 1968 we tried again. My team and I gave a new heart to a man called Philip Blaiberg. This time we dealt with the problem of rejection better. Philip lived for 19 months after the operation.

That operation was the second of my 165 heart transplants. Each time we did the operation, we learned more about how to improve the <u>survival rate</u>. The fifth person, a woman called Dorothy Fisher, lived for 12 years after the transplant. My sixth patient lived for 24 years after her operation.

All this was good. But transplanting a heart wasn't always the answer to a sick person's problem. I became interested in <u>artificial</u> heart-valves. Sometimes replacing a valve, not the whole heart, was a better way of solving a problem. This was especially true when children had heart problems.

There were problems again because some religious people and politicians didn't like the idea of artificial heart-valves. Some of them thought that using artificial valves was worse than transplanting human hearts! But for me, there was no problem. I remembered my little brother. I thought that everyone had the <u>right</u> to live.

◆ ◆ ◆

I was a famous person, with many famous friends. Film stars wanted to know me. But I continued with my work in heart surgery for as long as I could. When I stopped, in 1983, the reason was a medical one. I had arthritis in my hands. This medical <u>condition</u> made my hands very painful and I couldn't <u>operate</u> well on small organs.

I couldn't do operations, but I continued to speak on radio and TV. I wrote some books. I tried to help my colleagues by talking to the government. I talked to the politicians, but I disagreed with the government of South Africa about many things. I hated its <u>racist</u> attitude to people who didn't have white skin.

One day, when I was 78, I had a pain in my chest. On 2nd September 2001, my own heart stopped working.

The Life of Christiaan Barnard

1922   Christiaan Neethling Barnard was born on 8th November in Beaufort West, Western Cape, South Africa. Christiaan had four brothers. One brother, Abraham, died of a heart problem at the age of 5.

1940   Christiaan graduated from the Beaufort West High School.

1941   He began studying medicine, at the University of Cape Town's Medical School.

1945   He graduated from the University of Cape Town with Bachelor of Medicine and Bachelor of Surgery degrees.

1946–1950   Christiaan worked first at the Groote Schuur Hospital, Cape Town. He then worked as a family doctor in the town of Ceres, Western Cape.

1948   He married Aletta Gertruida Louw, a nurse. They later had two children, Andre and Deirdre.

1951   Christaan returned to Cape Town and worked at the City Hospital, and at the Groote Schuur Hospital.

1953 He completed his Master of Medicine degree and then he earned another degree, both at the University of Cape Town. The first kidney transplant was done in the United States in this year.

1956 Christiaan went to the USA to study heart surgery. While he was at the University of Minnesota, Minneapolis, he met Doctor Norman Shumway.

1958 He received a Master of Science degree in Surgery and then a Doctor of Philosophy degree from the University of Minneapolis. Christiaan returned to South Africa.

1959 Christiaan did the first kidney transplant in South Africa.

1967 With a team of 30 people, Christiaan did the first successful human–to–human heart transplant on Louis Washkansky. Washkansky lived for 18 more days.

1968 Christiaan did another heart transplant. The patient, Philip Blaiberg, lived for 19 months after surgery.

1969 Christiaan published a book about his life, *Christiaan Barnard: One Life*.

1971 He did a heart transplant on Dirk van Zyl, who then lived for 23 more years.

1977   He used an animal heart as a temporary transplant in a human patient.

1983   Christiaan developed arthritis in his hands and he stopped doing operations. He went to the Baptist Medical Centre in Oklahoma, to study what happens to bodies as people get older.

1993   He published his second book about his life, *The Second Life*.

1990–2000   Christiaan spent time in Austria, where he started the Christiaan Barnard Foundation for children. He often returned to his farm in Beaufort West, South Africa.

1997   His book, *The Donor*, was published.

2001   Christiaan died on 2nd September while he was on holiday in Paphos, Cyprus. He was 78 years old.

alchemy NOUN
a form of chemistry studied in
the Middle Ages, which tried to
discover ways to change ordinary
metals into gold

ambition NOUN
the feeling that you want very
much to do something in the
future

archaeology NOUN
the study of the past that is
done by examining the things
that remain, such as buildings
and tools

artificial ADJECTIVE
made by people, instead of being
made naturally

bacteria NOUN
very small living things that can
make people ill

barley NOUN
a crop whose seeds are used in
making food, beer and whisky

belief NOUN
a powerful feeling that
something is real or true

blister NOUN
a raised area of skin filled with
a liquid

campaign VERB
to do a number of actions over a
period of time in order to get a
particular result
NOUN
a series of actions to help
someone win an election

chemical NOUN
a substance that is used in a
chemical process or made by a
chemical process

compulsory ADJECTIVE
that someone or everyone
must do

condition NOUN
1 an illness or medical problem
2 the physical state of a place,
especially whether it is
comfortable and safe

cripple VERB
to stop someone from ever
moving their body normally again

depression NOUN
1 a state of mind in which you
are very sad and you feel that
you cannot enjoy anything
2 a time when there is very little
economic activity so that a lot of
people do not have jobs

dispensary NOUN
a place where medicines are
prepared and given out

drain NOUN
a pipe or opening that carries
dirty water away from a place

drug NOUN
a chemical that is used as a
medicine

elect VERB
to choose a person to do a
particular job by voting for them

election NOUN
a process in which people vote
to choose a person who will hold
an official position

establish VERB
to create an organization

extrovert NOUN
an active, lively person who
enjoys talking to people

factor NOUN
something that helps to produce
a result

family doctor NOUN
a doctor who does not specialize
in any particular area of medicine
and does not work in a hospital,
but who works in the community
and treats all types of illness

fever NOUN
a high temperature in your body
because you are ill

fund NOUN
an amount of money that people
save for a particular purpose

graduate VERB
to complete your studies at
school, college or university

heart failure NOUN
a serious medical condition in
which someone's heart stops
working properly, sometimes
causing death

hygiene NOUN
the practice of keeping yourself
and the things you use clean

identify VERB
to be able to say what
something is

identity NOUN
who a person is

infection NOUN
an illness that is caused by
bacteria

inject VERB
to put a substance such as a
medicine into someone's body
using a special type of needle

injection NOUN
medicine that someone puts into your body using a special type of needle

introvert NOUN
a quiet, shy person who finds it difficult to talk to people

involve
to be involved (in something)
PHRASE
to take part in an activity

kidney NOUN
one of the two organs in your body that remove waste liquid from your blood

malt VERB
to soak barley in water and then dry it in a hot oven, so that it can be used to make beer, whisky and other drinks

mayor NOUN
the person who is responsible for the government of a city or a town

mental ADJECTIVE
relating to the mind

mythology NOUN
a group of myths (= well-known stories), especially those from a particular country, religion or culture

negative ADJECTIVE
unpleasant or harmful

operate VERB
to cut open a patient's body in order to remove or repair part of it

operation NOUN
when a doctor cuts open a patient's body in order to remove or repair part of it

organ NOUN
a part of your body that has a particular purpose, for example your heart or stomach

parliament NOUN
the group of people who make or change the laws of some countries

patient NOUN
a person who receives medical treatment

personality NOUN
the qualities that make you different from other people

philosopher NOUN
a person who studies or writes about philosophy

philosophy NOUN
the study of ideas about the meaning of life

Poor Laws NOUN
a system of laws in Britain in the past which controlled how poor people could be helped

prevent VERB
to stop something from happening

protection NOUN
something that stops you from being harmed or damaged by something bad

psychologist NOUN
a person who studies the human mind and tries to explain why people behave in the way that they do

psychology NOUN
the study of the human mind and the reasons for people's behaviour

pus NOUN
a thick yellow liquid that forms when part of the body is infected

qualification NOUN
an examination you have passed that shows you are able to do a particular job

qualify VERB
to be fully trained to do a particular job

racist ADJECTIVE
believing that some people are better than others because they belong to a particular race

rash NOUN
an area of red spots that appears on your skin

religious ADJECTIVE
1 believing strongly in religion
2 connected with religion

right NOUN
something that you are allowed to do morally or by law

Royal Commission NOUN
a group of people that has been asked by the government, king or queen to find out and make a formal report about an important question

statistic NOUN
a fact that is expressed in numbers

statistician NOUN
a person who studies statistics or who works using statistics

sue VERB
to start a legal case against someone, usually in order to get money from them because they have harmed you

support NOUN
actions or words that show that
you agree with someone
VERB
to help someone because you
want them to succeed

surgeon NOUN
a doctor who is specially trained
to perform operations

surgery NOUN
a process in which a doctor cuts
open a patient's body in order
to repair or remove part of it

survival rate NOUN
the number of people who
remain alive after a particular
illness or dangerous event

survive VERB
to remain alive after an illness or
dangerous event

thesis (theses) NOUN
a long piece of writing based on
your own ideas and research that
you do as part of a university
degree

train VERB
to learn the skills that you need
in order to do something

training NOUN
the process of learning the skills
that you need in order to do
something

training college NOUN
a college where people are
trained to do a particular job,
such as nursing or teaching

transplant VERB
to replace a part of a person's
body in a medical operation
NOUN
a medical operation in which a
part of a person's body is replaced

treat VERB
to try to make a patient
well again

treatment NOUN
medical attention that is given
to someone to try to make
them well

unconscious ADJECTIVE
not awake and not aware of what
is happening around you
because of illness or an injury

unconscious mind NOUN
the part of your mind that
contains feelings and ideas that
you do not know about or
cannot control

vaccine NOUN
a substance containing a very
small amount of the thing that
causes a particular disease. It is
given to people to prevent them
from getting that disease.

vaccination NOUN
a treatment in which someone is
given a vaccine to prevent them
from getting a disease

valve NOUN
a small piece of tissue in your
heart which controls the flow of
blood and keeps it flowing in one
direction only

virus NOUN
a very small living thing that can
enter your body and make you ill

wound VERB
to damage someone's body with
a gun or something sharp
NOUN
damage to part of your body
caused by a gun or something
sharp like a knife

wounded ADJECTIVE
having suffered damage to part
of your body because of a gun
or something sharp